Rabindranath Tagore

Art by Jaikar

Suppose I became
a champa flower,
just for fun?

And grew on a
branch high up
that tree.

Suppose I shook in the wind
with laughter?

And danced upon the
newly budded leaves.

Would you know me, Ma?

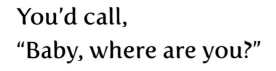

You'd call,
"Baby, where are you?"

And I'd laugh to myself
and keep quite quiet.

I would slyly open
my petals and watch
you at work.

When after your bath,
with wet hair spread
on your shoulders,

You'd walk under
the champa tree to the little court
where you say your prayers,

You'd notice
the scent of the flower,
but not know
that it came from me.

After the midday meal
you would sit at the window
reading the Ramayana,

And the tree's shadow
would fall over your hair
and your lap.

I would fling
my wee little shadow
on to the page of your book,
just where you were reading.

But would you guess
that it was
the tiny shadow
of your little child?

When in the evening
you'd go to the cowshed
with the lighted lamp
in your hand,

I'd suddenly drop
on to the earth again
and be your own baby
once more,

And beg you
to tell me a story.

"Where have you been,
my naughty child?"

"I won't tell you, Ma,"
I'd say then!

eat, read, sleep, play...

What do you think of when you look at the clocks below?

....
....
....

....
....
....

paste your photo

....
....
....

....
....
....

shadows speak!

On a bright sunny day, go out with a friend and trace his shadow at different times of the day.

Can you guess the time of the day just by looking at the shadows?

Know
Gurudev

Rabindranath Tagore, the youngest child of his parents had fourteen siblings.

From the time he was a child, little Rabi, as he was called, loved reading, writing, music and arts, much like the rest of his family. Rabi and his brothers and sisters played in the outdoors a lot. They wrestled, swam in rivers and walked through the hills near their home.

He wrote many patriotic songs, including our national anthem, *Jana Gana Mana*. In appreciation of all his work, Gandhiji lovingly gave him the title, Gurudev and that is how the world remembers him to this day.

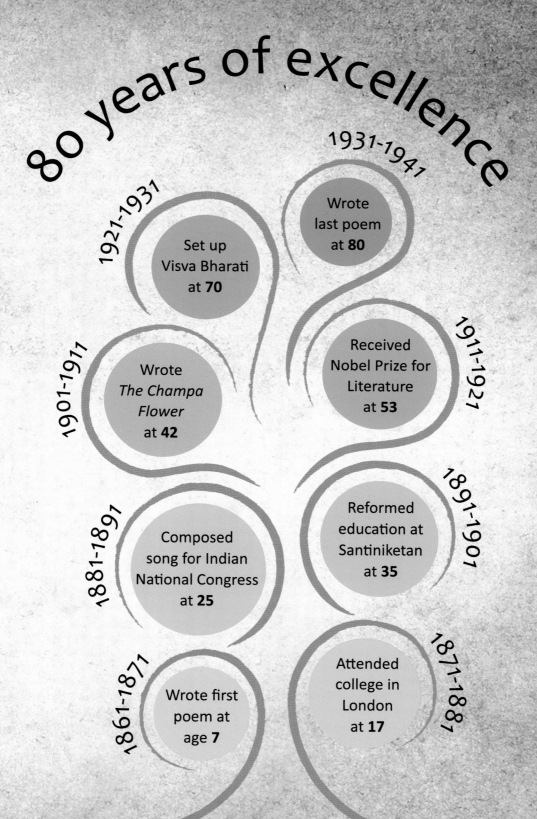

Jaikar Marur completed his mechanical engineering from NITK, Surathkal, and went on to learn animation at the National Institute of Design. He loves drawing, painting, illustrating and reading folk and fairy tales. His heroes range from Newton and Feynman in Physics to Michelangelo and Rubens in Art. He hopes to paint like his art heroes some day.

Therefore Design is a Pune-based, multidisciplinary design house that offers sevices in various fields.

KATHA

First published © Katha, 2012
Copyright © Katha, 2012
Text copyright © Katha, 2012
Illustrations copyright © Jaikar Marur, 2012
All rights reserved. No part of this book may be reproduced or utilized in any form without the prior written permission of the publisher.
Printed at RaveIndia, New Delhi
ISBN 978-93-82454-00-7

KATHA is a registered nonprofit devoted to enhancing the joys of reading amongst children and adults. Katha schools are situated in the slums and streets of Delhi and tribal villages of Arunachal Pradesh.
A3 Sarvodaya Enclave, Sri Aurobindo Marg
New Delhi 110 017
Phone: 4141 6600 . 4182 9998 . 2652 1752
Fax: 2651 4373
E-mail: marketing@katha.org, Website: www.katha.org

Ten percent of sales proceeds from this book will support the quality education of children studying in Katha schools.
Katha regularly plants trees to replace the wood used in the making of its books.